T0195848

A CROWDED HEAD

Living

With

Dissociate

Identity

Disorder

By Billie Marie

To order additional copies of this book, contact:
Xlibris
844-714-8691
www.Xlibris.com
Orders@Xlibris.com

ISBN: Softcover   979-8-3694-0491-1
         EBook   979-8-3694-0492-8

Library of Congress Control Number: 2023914758

Print information available on the last page

Rev. date: 08/09/2023

This book is a compilation of poems and introspective thoughts of Billie Marie and some of the other Selves that were drawn out over the years in sessions with our therapist Dr. Cynthia. I hope this assortment of writings will give the reader an understanding of the struggles of people with Dissociate Identity and gender issues, and, for readers who find something of their own lives in this book, maybe I can show them that they are not alone and that there is hope for a better life.

This book could not have been written without the support of two especially important women. I certainly would not be the person I am today without their presence in my life.

The first of these wonderful women is Debra, my wife of more than 26 years. Her unfailing support through our most challenging times has been an inspiration to me and is the definition of true love. I would have understood if she had left after the first 18 years of marriage having found out I was not the man she had first fallen in love with, but, instead, accepted me as the deeply confused and flawed person that I am.

The other woman to whom I owe special thanks is Dr. Cynthia, my psychotherapist of more than 8 years. Through her guidance and support I have been transformed from a man suffering from a lifetime of depression and recurring thoughts of suicide into a person who has finally found real happiness. Dr. Cynthia is a true professional who has never failed to focus my attention in the right direction. By encouraging me to write my thoughts down in diaries and poems she has helped me bring out the other Selves I never suspected were buried in my head. As each Self emerged over the past few years and revealed themselves to me, Dr. Cynthia has helped me understand how they fit into my life.

I am truly lucky and grateful to have such strong women to turn to when the daily ups and downs of life leave me confused and wondering who I am, but also through the darkest times when life doesn't feel worth living.

Washing away the layers of pain
that once flooded my Soul.
The decades of isolation
that kept me from feeling whole.
The person that I was
walked through life alone.
That person that I was
may soon be gone.

Seeing life through another's eyes;
finding hope in where my future lies,
uncovering the woman
hidden deep inside.

I am the woman that in my past
I was forced to hide!

Coming out

I pray that when that day comes
you can look at me and not judge.
I will come to you with my heart laid bare.
Vulnerable.
In need of your love and compassion
as I make my way along a new road
I have found before me.
I hope you see that the person on the inside
is more than the man you thought you knew.

My coming out is as much a surprise to me
as it is to you.
The truth is I've never known myself.
I've never known how many hidden Selves
I've kept buried inside.
So many other persons with emotions
I've never allowed myself to feel.

I pray you will open your mind
as you see I'm not the person
you always thought I was.
And please forgive me
I never meant to deceive anyone
All I ever wanted was to be understood and loved.

CHAPTER 1

Growing Pains

We all come into this world with a perfect Soul.
Our Soul is each person's inner being.
It is who we are.
It is unchanging and always good.
We as individuals are not defined by our Soul,
but by our personality.
Our Self.

While each of us come into this world
with our own personality it is not unchanging,
but is influenced by the world around us
and by our own mind and body.
Our Self becomes a reflection of the world
in which we live and our place in that world.

What happened to that little boy
whose life began with so much promise?
He had his whole world in front of him.
His whole life waiting to begin.

It's sad how life can be so cruel.
The pain can cut so deep.
You lost faith in yourself
and in your prayers for a better life.
All you wanted was to be heard
but for years your struggle continued.
Your childhood dreams have slowly disappeared
replaced by feelings of anger, pain and regret
as you built a wall around your heart.

My impediment
I relive it everyday.
Live it with the same pain
I felt the first time.
It's always the same.
Never changes.
Never gets better.
Never goes away.

Is that a clue to why I am
the way I am?
I am not like everyone else!
You'll never understand.
I'm not what you want me to be.
I'm not the man I should be!
That's why I live my own life.
I live in my own world.
A world you'll never see.

I felt the loneliness
of being an outsider
in the family I grew up in.
I knew the frustration
of being misunderstood
by the people closest to me.
I felt my spirit shrink
til I became a shadow of myself.
I searched my heart
to find someone else
better prepared to take my place.

On my own I find strength
from the people in my head.
Around others I melt into the crowd.
Where do I find comfort?
In my loneliness
I dreamt of being Someone else.
A life begun with so much promise
turned into so much pain.

I'm struggling with myself today,
feeling helpless and alone.
Depression is taking hold again,
paralyzing my Soul.
I cannot control the feelings
that others have for me,
I can only try to show them my best
and trust they like who they see;
if they choose not to be a friend,
that's on them, not me.

I need to get past my anger.
I need to work through
these feelings of rejection.
I need to find the good in my heart.

I'm struggling with myself today;
wanting to become the better part of me.
I feel her in my heart,
she's buried deep inside.

Living with one foot in reality,
how can I keep my sanity?
I'm so much happier
in my own little world.

Living on the edge of reality
is there any room for me?
I feel my sanity slipping away...
How do I find my way
in the "real world"?

Living in your rigid reality
is eroding my stability;
forcing my Selves to find comfort
in a place inside your world.

How do I show you my reality?
Can you accept me as I am?
The thought of being like me
is so foreign to everything you believe.

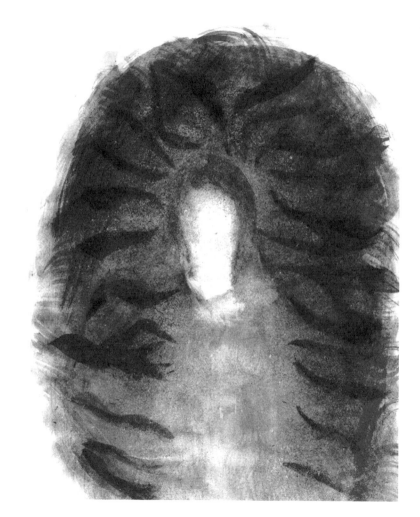

Feeling paranoid and lost in my head.
Losing my mind...
Wishing I was dead!
Feeling so alone.
Wishing I was dead!
I want to shut the world out.
Let me be alone.
I just want to be alone!

How do I fight these thoughts of suicide?
I can't live this way!
I can't go on being this man.
I'm losing control.
Living alone.
Losing my Soul.

In Support of Suicide

Life can be so unfair
and many times
the people in our lives can be so cold.
They cannot understand how we became this person.
They cannot be bothered to listen when we speak.
And yet they go on judging us
for our weaknesses and faults.
They compare their lives to ours.
They say we should be more like them.
They don't see how we are different.
Why do they think they have all the answers?!
You need to go to church!
You need to pray to God!
Take your medication!
If only life could be so simple.
And so someday
when I finally find peace of mind,
they'll tell themselves I was selfish.
They'll say I never thought of the people I left behind.

I'm taking my medication
while I put my brain on vacation.
I'm not losing my mind,
I'm just letting it find
whatever place,
whatever world,
will give me peace of mind.

I can't stand to feel normal,
this world is too stiff and formal.
...Maybe my problem is hormonal...
I've become bored being a man.
I want to be a woman whenever I can.

I've wanted to live an alternate life
since I was a child;
just let my fantasies run wild.
Maybe I've lived alone too long
in my own world gone wrong,
but this is how I cope
when I know there is no other hope.
So now I take my medication
and put my brain on vacation.

Billie Marie

How can I take my own life
when we only get one goodbye?
We only get one goodbye...
and sooner or later
their memory of me runs out.
So that's why I'll never take
my own life!

I have too many memories
still to make.
So much of life left to live.
I'm not ready to give in yet.
So that's why I'll hang on as long as I can.

The only thing worse than being forgotten
is being forgotten too soon!
Everyone wants to be remembered
by the people in their life,
but memories can be short-lived;
frozen in time by those left behind.

So how can I take my own life?
When we only get one goodbye.
I need to be here for the people that love me!

CHAPTER 2

Dissociate Identity Disorder

Separation of the mind from the Soul.
Ungrounded.
Losing one's true Self.
Living a life of fantasies and alternate realities.
Feeling lost and disconnected from others.
Out of touch with one's own feelings.
Slipping into and out of Selves subconsciously.
Self-loathing and depression.
Feeling useless and insignificant.
Lifelong loneliness.
Clinging to regrets of the past
and fear of the future.

The Narrator controls my brain,
the Overseer watches over me
and keeps me sane.
I am too many people
to be given control
over my own life.

This person you see
was born with too many flaws,
his growth broke too many natural laws.

At an early age this person was damaged;
our Soul took over to save what could be salvaged.
So now that boy who thought he was in control
has finally learned the truth;
he was left behind early in his youth!

This person who came to life so happily as a boy
became broken and fragmented til his life lost all its joy.

So now the Narrator takes control...

The Narrator

I am not the person in control.
But I am the person
above all my others.
I am male and female.
I am everyone in me
at the same moment.

While I am all my Selves
I also speak about them
as if they are someone separate.
They are not complete people.
They are only fragments
of a splintered mind
just as I am only one of that same mind.
They are all parts of me,
but together they don't make me whole
they only make me different.

I am anyone of us when I need to be,
and yet I'm still not sure which of us
is really me!
I am each of us because I am not strong enough
to be only one.

A Crowded Head

I enjoy talking out loud
when I'm alone.
So tell me who's listening?
Who else is home?

I have a crowded head.
All these friends.
All these realities.
But, I still have to ask the question...
Do I even need to mention?
I know I'm not alone.
They've been there all my life,
and yet I never knew their names.

I enjoy talking out loud...
when I'm alone.
All my friends are here with me
in our own little worlds.

Hidden in rooms in my head
my other selves live their lives.
Sometimes they find a way out
through a door left unlocked.
Maybe they're the crazy people
that make me feel unnormal.
Maybe they're the reason
I think I'm someone
other than who I am.
How do I keep them hidden inside?
But wait!
Why would I want to?
Why would I want to go back
to the life I lived before?
Show me the doors so I can leave them open.
It's time to let them all out.
I want to lose control!
I need to let myself go!

Early in life I learned to play it safe,
I became that boy.
But was he who I really was?
Was he who I was meant to be?
I hid my softer emotions away
showing only anger,
feeling only regret and pain.
Always hiding the better side of me
and keeping my emotions deep inside.

I became that boy.
I became my own protector.
My shield against the world.
I became that boy
not to feel love,
but to protect my Soul from pain.
I feared rejection more than anything.
So, I became that boy and let my heart turn cold.

Why do I need to feel this pain?
Why do I still need to hurt inside?
What will it take to let it all go?
Move on from my past...
Find a way to grow...

I will heal myself.
Move forward.
Set my spirit free.

I carry the scars of my youth
though I keep them hidden in my mind.
I appear normal to the world
to give you all nothing to find.

My mind has been drained.
Nothing left to feel.
Nothing left to say.

Coming down from a rollercoaster of emotions;
Finding myself just going through the motions.
This week my father was laid to rest,
the strength of my spirit was put to the test.
I'm still here.
I'm still alive.
But when I lost my dad
a part of me died.
I know I never lived up to his expectations
yet he loved me just the same.
The boy on the outside never became a man
overwhelmed by life I did the best I can.
The woman on the inside, freed by our Soul,
fights to become whole.
This woman longed to find acceptance,
but our world has suddenly changed
and now it's too late for a second chance.

Where do you go
when you can't get away
from the person
you least want to see?
Where can I go
when I can't get away from me?

I'm a twin bound by my mind
to someone I can't stand to be.
I have a life to live.
I have so much to give.
So much to give...
So let me grow.
Let me live.
Let me start over again.

CHAPTER 3

Questions

My Soul is separate from my selves.
My Soul is genderless.
Each of my selves was formed
to protect my Soul from outside forces.
Each self formed at different times
Under different circumstances,
Some living on,
Some disappearing over time.
All leaving their own memories
on my Soul.

Looking at that person in the mirror.
That face...
Those eyes...
Looking back at me.
Who is he?
Is he really me?!
All I know is I don't want to be
that man looking back at me.

I don't want to be that man.

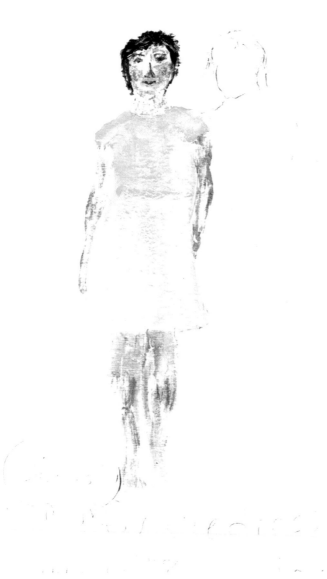

I'm trapped here in the moment.
Living in two worlds.
Caught between boy and girl.
I'm a trans in limbo
unable to get a push
to let myself go.

I'm taking another step forward
while stuck here between two worlds.
Caught between boy and girl.
How do I get past trans in limbo?
Push me through the door
so I can let the boy go.
I'm a trans in limbo
but I can't change
from the person I am.
And yet the woman inside
longs to set herself free.

She called my art pornography!
Too bad she doesn't see
I'm just revealing the woman inside me
caught in a moment of intimacy.
Her portrait, so dramatic,
shows the image of a woman
so enigmatic.

I feel her heartbeat just below the surface
as I peel away the layers of my maleness.
The blinders are removed from the man I had been.
The curtain is drawn to reveal the woman within.

She called my art pornography
because at first glance
it wasn't what she expected to see.
But now I'm guided by the woman inside me.
Born in a world of a different reality,
her most intimate thoughts become my fantasies.

My art is a mirror of my heart
and a reflection of the Selves hidden within.
As I allow them each day to take more of my Soul
their spirits inside me become a little more whole.
I grasp a little harder on something to hold
as I need them all to become more whole.

Why do I not need to look pretty?
Why is it ok to look like that man?
What does that say about me?
Who does that tell me I am?
I'm still lost and confused.
Still don't know who I am.
I still need to feel abused.
Still want to be used.

I don't want to be the man I am.
So how do I become the woman
I want to be?
I wouldn't be this way if I loved myself.
I wish I could become someone else.
Even I don't want to be around me.
But the real me doesn't belong to this reality.
The real me is someone most people will never see.
I keep the real me buried deep inside.
That way I don't feel a need to hide
It doesn't matter who's on the outside
I've always been all about me.
The rest of the world, well, they're still there.

I wanted to smile today
but I couldn't convince myself.
I just wasn't in the mood.
The person in charge
wouldn't be consoled.
I don't know how to change his mind.
He's stubborn and can't be told.

Must be his depression
that makes him feel this way.
It settled in his brain like a virus
and just won't go away.
Will they ever find a cure?!
They tried to treat him with medication,
but they just don't know for sure.

Later today I'll be someone else.
I know that she will smile.
I won't have to convince her.
But him?
I really don't know.
He just won't change.

Dr. Cynthia,

Of course, I'm not the person
who would say those things,
or think those things,
or be that way.
The truth can be hard to find
when buried deep beneath decades
of loneliness, anger, pain, and regret.

So now I finally see what you meant.
The answers are hard to find
when we're so closely connected,
so closely tied
to our other selves' thoughts and emotions
and their wishes and dreams.
I finally understand everything you told me.
It's now so obvious.
Why could I not see it before?
You know me better than I know myself.
I was in denial for so long!

I heard a voice
that woke me
from my sleep.
A woman's voice
that took me
from my dreams.
She sounded like
my guardian angel,
but my lover
said it wasn't her.
She said I woke her
as she slept.
So, the voice I heard
came from my head.
I heard that voice before;
a siren from my mind
waking me to warn me,
or, maybe prepare me
for a change in me
soon to be.

I heard a voice that woke me from my sleep.
A woman's voice that took me from my dreams.
A woman's voice!
Another part of me setting herself free...

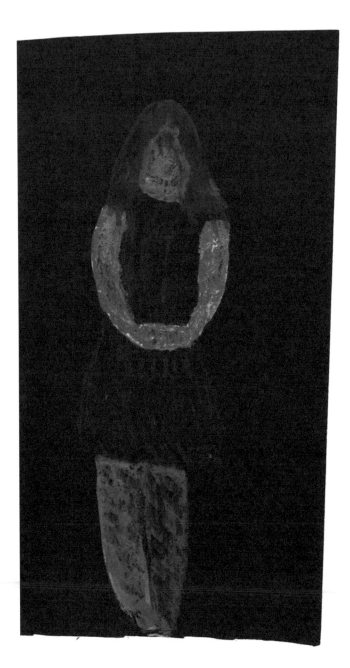

I have become my own interpretation of a woman.
I never made it as a man.
Reality was not kind.
I lost my way…
What more can I say?

I knew how to be a boy.
It all came naturally
as anyone would expect.
But I never understood
what should come next.
I was lost.
Locked inside a world
I could never outgrow.
Looking for answers
to life on my own.
I found relief from the stress
in my world
through fantasies of becoming a girl.

Layers of Selves
piled atop each other.
Decades of layers
one upon each one.
Pieces of a puzzle
jumbled and misplaced.

Am I a man wanting to be a woman?
Or a woman struggling to break free
from a person never meant to be?

I need to find the answers.
I want to make sense of this life.
A life filled with so much pain
and confusion.
A life that made no sense
as I lived each day.

CHAPTER 4

Finding Myself

Each of my Selves have their own purpose,
but can they become whole over time?
Can I become a new person
from the separate and independent Selves
that were formed to protect my Soul?
...and what became of that young girl
that has haunted my mind since puberty?

Little Joanie.
Her spirit hit me like a hurricane.
Taking over my mind
and changing my life.
I needed to become this
young girl before
I could free the woman in my Soul.

Little Joanie.
Her spirit overwhelmed me,
taking over my senses,
(and common sense).
The innocence she brought to my life!
Her sense of wonder
that filled my heart.
Her laughter and tears
took away years of pain and despair.

Little Joanie.
Her presence in this old body
and her feelings of joy
and sense of wonder
opened my eyes
and led me to a better life.

My worlds are colliding.
Crashing and burning.
Exploding in my head.
The anger of this man testing his limits.
Suddenly I feel a calming presence...
The patience of Carol Ann takes over.

In these times of stress, she tells me:
"Relax a moment.
Take a breath.
Let the anger pass.
Take another breath and begin again."

The man feels the urgency of the moment.
The need to act before it's too late.
He feels the world crashing down.
Once again Carol comes through saying:
"Take time to let this pass...
bring it down a bit.
Take a deep breath,
we can make this work."

Carol Ann saves me from myself.
So why am I still him?
Why am I so afraid to come out
and be the person best for me?!

Don't talk to me sexy
about getting rough.
I don't want to hear it!
Don't talk to me about being
badass tough.
I don't care!
You don't know me,
I can walk away.
Nothing you say
can make me wanna stay.

Don't think you can impress me
with all the secrets
you think you know.
I've heard them all before.
Next thing you'll see is me
walking out the door.

Don't talk to me sexy
about getting rough.
Don't tell me you can't get enough
because I know you'll be looking for someone else,
anyway,
the first time I turn you away.
I'm looking for someone
to be the one
to light a spark in my heart.
Billie

She took over my mind,
now she owns my Soul.
That's ok.
I'll give them up willingly.
If she can steer me in the
right direction, I'm all hers.
When I think of all the times
I nearly drove myself into a ditch
I can now let someone else drive
and take me in a new direction.

Remember when I wore that blue dress?
I loved the way it let me feel.
So much inside me I needed to reveal.

Remember how I loved that blue dress?
I would have done anything for you!
The love I felt was pure and true.
You were everything to me.

If only I could've made you see...
I wore it for you and no one else!

I came to life when I wore that blue dress.
I wanted to be just like you!
I could do anything you could do,
but when I wore that blue dress
I could be myself.
I left behind everything else
that made me feel like you.

When I wore that blue dress
I showed you a side you never knew
buried so deep inside of you.
I tried so hard to awaken you
but you never had a clue!

I want to be Audrey Hepburn.
I want to be cute.
I want to be sexy.
I want to be desirable.
That woman's charm was so ...
Undeniable.

I want to be Audrey.
I want to have her style!
I want to have her class!
I want to have her poise!
Her grace...
Her perfect nose...
Her perfect face.
I want to be Audrey Hepburn!

I want to wear her clothes.
I want to wear whatever I want.
I want to wear whatever
that woman wears whenever
she wants to be a woman.

I want to be Audrey.

How do I start the conversation?
How do I tell someone
who used to be
close to me
I can no longer be
the man as they remember me?
What do I say
knowing they
will never, ever,
see me the same?
I just don't know where to begin.

So where do I start?
How much should I open my heart?
Maybe I could talk about
all the ways my life went wrong.
How I always felt I could never belong.

I think it's best to take it slow,
give the words time to take hold.
Let them see how content I've become
and let them feel my inner glow.

In my own world - even
in a crowd

If I come out
I won't expect
anyone to understand.
I'll do it for myself and
not for them.
If I come out
I know I'll be out there
on my own.
I'll come out for the person
I've become.
I'll do it for myself
and no one else.
Will it seem selfish?
Will it be all about me?
...Maybe...
But I'll decide when it's time!
And in a way that's right for me.
I am not a selfish person.
I won't make it all about me.
I can't forget the feelings
of the family that loves me,
but, if I come out,
I'll need to be strong
because I know I'll be
on my own!

This is my moment to shine!
...So why do I hesitate?
Why do I wait for a voice
to give me the ok?
The door is open...
The time has come
to step into the sunlight
of a new day!

Why does he still have a need
to hold me back?!
I know he's here to protect us,
but the time is now!

This is my moment to shine,
but there's no need to tell the world.
No need to send out announcements.
Let them find out by accident...
or a slip of the tongue...
Does it matter how it happens?
The time has come.
This is my moment to shine!

Printed in the United States
by Baker & Taylor Publisher Services